Finding Time for Your Scholarly Writing

A Short Guide

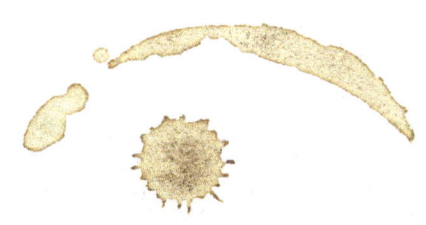

Jo VanEvery, PhD

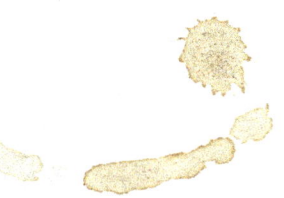

Finding Time for Your Scholarly Writing

Short Guides, vol 2

ISBN: 978-1-912040-70-4 (pb) 978-1-912040-69-8 (ebook)

Cover Design: Amy Crook

Jo Van Every

Table of Contents

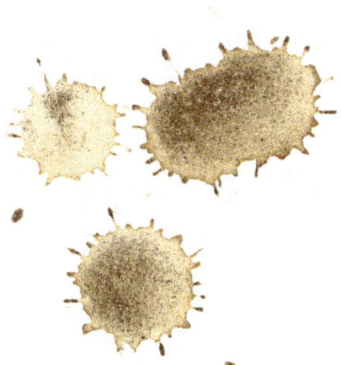

JO VAN EVERY

Everyone Struggles With Making Time for Writing

There is nothing wrong with you. You are not lacking willpower, planning ability, or motivation. Finding and protecting time for writing, especially during the parts of the year when you are teaching, is difficult.

While writing is a core activity for academics, you have a lot of other demands on your time and energy, many of them equally important. Those other activities often have more immediate impacts and involve other people in more immediate ways. Someone will notice if you do not turn up to teach, or if you are underprepared when you do, in a way that is just not true for your writing on any particular occasion. The fact that writing may be more important to your career can get twisted so that it seems selfish to devote time to it. The impact on other scholars, students, or anyone else happens a long time after the act of doing the work, and the relationship between sitting down to write and some future impact is rarely direct. It's more like flapping butterfly wings and weather events in distant places.

Some of your other work has the benefit of immediate outcomes that you can tick off a list in a way that writing doesn't always have. Scholarly writing projects are long term projects, with few real milestones. In the first *Short Guide* in this series, *The Scholarly Writing Process*, I argue that writing begins with exploring your curiosity and extends through identifying possible outputs and refining them for publication. Parts of the process don't look like writing at all, and yet reading and deep thinking are crucial to good scholarship.

While some writing advice makes a distinction between pre-writing tasks and writing, I find it more helpful to think of writing as encompassing everything that moves your projects forward. Sometimes, moving your project forward requires you to do tasks that seem like not-writing: reading, reanalyzing some data, freewriting about your ideas, etc. It's hard enough to find time to write. I don't want your project to get stalled because your gremlins are telling you that you can't do this kind of work during your writing time. If you are doing a particular task as a way of calming your fear that what you have to say isn't worth saying, that's procrastination. The line between the two isn't always clear but you will get better at spotting the difference with practice.

I advocate establishing a writing practice. Make writing something you do regularly, rather than something you do only when you have a specific output to produce. The relationship between time spent focused on your writing project and visible outcomes isn't direct. Some days it feels like you have accomplished practically nothing, but struggling with your ideas impacts what you are able to write another day. The writing process will also generate new ideas which more writing will help you articulate and develop. In that sense, it never ends, though you will decide that particular outputs of the process are finished and can be submitted for publication.

I also advocate making writing a priority when you plan. This is not selfish. The idea of blocking time for writing will seem less daunting when you consider the different kinds of time available. While certain kinds of writing may be impossible in certain kinds of time, there will always be something you can do to stay engaged with the writing process.

This *Short Guide* is structured around three kinds of time: full days, longish periods that are less than a full day, and short snatches of time. I've kept it short so you can spend your time writing instead of reading about writing. I begin with a bit more explanation of what I mean by "writing practice" and some thoughts on planning and goal setting. Then I look at each type of time, examining both what can be achieved and how you can fit it into your workload. Annotated references can be found at the end of the book organized by chapter.

Read the whole book straight through once to get a sense of how it all fits together. My hope is that you will then come back to specific sections as you need them:

for ideas when writing time seems impossible to find, for reassurance that whatever time you can find will be worth using, and for help making the best use of the time you have.

What is a writing practice?

The term "writing" (as I've argued in more detail in *The Scholarly Writing Process*) refers to both the process of translating the ideas in your head into words on a page and to the products of that process. Writing-as-process isn't merely an act of transcription designed to produce writing-as-product. Writing is a cognitive process in which you develop and articulate your ideas. A lot of work goes into finding the right words, sorting your thoughts, and focusing your argument.

Because of this, it is not helpful to think of writing as something you do only when you have a particular product in mind. Not everything you write will be something you want to share with others. It is not a waste of time to write:

- things that will never become conference papers, or articles
- unsuccessful grant proposals
- book proposals that you decide not to submit to a publisher

All writing is worthwhile if it helps move your thinking forward. Sometimes "moving your thinking forward" looks like going off on a tangent, or even failing.

You are a writer not only because you can point to things you have written (and published), but also because writing is how you process ideas and make them intelligible to yourself and others. It is much more helpful to think of writing as a practice, analogous to a yoga practice or a spiritual practice. Once established, a writing practice is not another item on your to-do list but a fundamental part of what it means to be you. Establishing a writing practice helps build your confidence that the work you want to do (and love doing, even when you hate it) is real work. You will be confident that you deserve the time to do this work.

Many aspects of writing, as both process and product, are out of your control. Establishing a writing practice builds your trust in the creative process. Trust that others will read your work. Trust that others will be inspired by your work. Trust that others will acknowledge your role in the creation of that knowledge. Trust that your institution will recognize and accept the outputs of your creative process.

Even with an effective practice, writing will often be difficult. You will:

- need strategies to overcome inertia and get into flow
- struggle with particular sections
- need to revise what you write (probably several times)

It will take longer than you think, and this will be frustrating. Some days you will write a lot. Other days it will feel like pouring molasses on a cold day.

A writing practice is not something you figure out once and never have to think about again. A particular writing strategy may work well for you for a while and then stop working. What works today may or may not work tomorrow. You are not the same every time you sit down to write. Your ability to focus and to undertake the complex cognitive processes involved in writing varies for a number of reasons. It may be cyclical, reflecting seasonal changes in the quantity and quality of daylight and the attendant impact on your mood, or the broader cycles of variation in your context determined by the academic calendar and your stage of career. Changes may also reflect the variations in context from one day to the next, in terms of your other activities, your health, your level of energy, and so on.

Your goal in establishing a practice is not to find the magic combination of moves that will result in more publications. Your goal is to be a writer. Your writing practice needs flexibility built in to cope with daily variation and requires periodic evaluation to ensure that it still works for you over longer periods of time.

When your main job doesn't pay for writing

This *Short Guide* is for you if your scholarly writing is important to you even if it's not your primary focus or part of how you earn your living. It is unreasonable to assume that the only people engaged in scholarly writing are those employed full time as academics in positions where research and writing are part of their job description. Remember, there are lots of writers out there who have a day job to pay the rent. The fact that they write different kinds of things to what you write is not important.

This guide is also for you if you

- are employed as an academic in an institution with a strong focus on teaching and little or no support for research

- have a teaching focused contract in an institution that also has academics with different kinds of contracts that also include research

- have a very heavy teaching load and perhaps a lot of advising and other service responsibilities

- have a precarious and poorly paid teaching contract, or are patching together multiple such contracts to make ends meet

- are employed in a non-academic position within a university or college

- are employed outside of the education sector altogether, whether or not that job is closely related to your research and writing interests

- have a job that involves writing and publishing for very different audiences or in a different style to some of the scholarly writing you also want to do

- are out of the labour market, perhaps caring for children or elderly relatives, but want to keep up your scholarly writing for various reasons

Scholarly writing is meaningful and important to you. The way you use the three kinds of writing time may be very different depending on your employment situation. Your goal is to find a way to develop a writing practice that works for you.

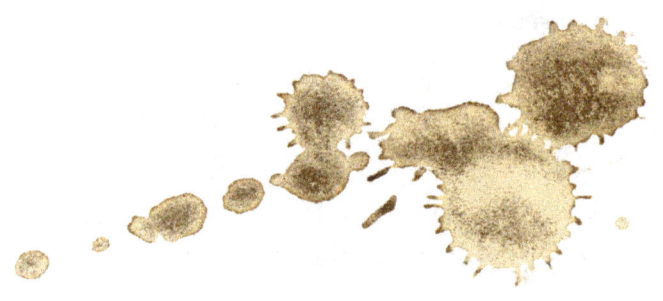

Planning to Include Writing

How you include writing in your plans will vary but you must plan to write or it won't happen. If you have an academic position, whether short term or permanent, writing is one of several responsibilities: teaching, meetings, advising students, and so on. Your workload is heavy. The demands of each of these vary considerably over the year, and even week to week during term time. If writing is something you do in addition to a different kind of job or responsibility then you can consider writing alongside other activities you are engaged in outside of work. The limits on the time and energy available for these activities is frustrating.

Plans reduce stress

Overwhelm and stress are only partly due to the number of things you have on your to-do list. The primary contributor to stress is lack of control over your time and energy. The fear that you are going to drop a ball is a big part of that stress. A good plan can significantly reduce the stress, even if you still have a lot to do.

There is a strong temptation to act as if you have no control over your time or your activities. This is not true. Some of your work is non-negotiable and possibly scheduled by someone else. Even with those constraints, you have a lot more autonomy over what you do, and how and when you do it, than many professionals. What you don't have is a boss and a departmental culture that will make those decisions for you.

You need to take personal responsibility for your workload. That means taking responsibility for all the things you will not get to. It also means making tough decisions about whether or not it is worth taking the time to do a particular task to a higher standard. If scholarly writing is something you do in addition to your paid work, you have less time but more control. You will still have tough decisions to make, but they will be about which activities are a priority for you outside of work. Autonomy means taking responsibility for making the wrong call. You have good judgement. You will make mistakes, but they are probably not going to be fatal.

Plans reduce decision fatigue and anxiety

A very important reason to establish a writing practice is to reduce the energy you expend on things like making decisions and being anxious so that you have more energy to spend on thinking and writing.

Making decisions is one of the most energy intensive things we do. An effective practice will incorporate a strategy for making writing the default activity in certain time slots, thus reducing the number of decisions you make about when to write and for how long. You will also need a strategy for deciding what to write so that when you sit down, you can get into the actual writing more quickly.

Anxiety and worry also use a lot of energy. The most common worry is that you aren't doing enough. Your to-do list never gets shorter. Things get added to it all the time. This has nothing to do with whether you are doing enough. You are a competent person who gets a lot done. Set reasonable goals. Keep your focus on how much you get done. Look for evidence that your projects are moving forward. Consciously review your accomplishments regularly.

Elements of a good plan

A good plan has three important elements: priorities, boundaries, and slack.

> priority (noun): 1. The fact or condition of being earlier in time or of preceding something else. 2. Precedence in order, rank, or dignity; the right to receive attention, supplies, etc., before others.

To make something a priority does not mean that you will spend more time on it than anything else. It means that it is most important. It means that you will allocate resources (of time, energy, etc) to it before you allocate resources to other things.

If writing is a priority for you, you will find or make time to do it. You are not being selfish. No one else is going to make time for your writing. Consider what is reasonable, given your other responsibilities, and give those resources to your writing before other things, especially low priority things.

Boundaries enable you to balance your various different responsibilities and priorities. The easiest way to mark boundaries is to schedule blocks of time in your calendar. You may resist scheduling everything because it feels restricting. I encourage you to try it. You may find that having a schedule actually feels more free. A schedule also reduces decision fatigue and allays anxiety about whether you are getting to everything.

You will need some slack in your plans. Stuff will come up – extra meetings, illness, an opportunity you can't imagine now. You can't plan for everything. Slack enables you to minimize disruption and keep your commitments to your priority things.

The foundation of your writing practice is self-care in the most basic sense. You need to eat properly, get enough sleep, and exercise regularly to ensure that your body has enough energy. Do not skimp on this to make time for writing. Your higher cognitive functions are not effective when you are malnourished and sleep deprived. Your brain functions much better with lots of movement. That said, you can work on improving this foundation of self-care in parallel to establishing a writing practice.

Planning will be an iterative process. You will have to make difficult decisions about how much time you really have and how much you can accomplish. You may have to tweak your plan several times to get the balance right. You may not be able to do the same amount weekly. Work with what you have.

A writing practice is not something you figure out once and never have to think about again. Your goal is to find a way to develop a writing practice that works for you. Determine how much time you can reasonably allocate to writing, consider the three types of writing time, schedule a combination of those types in your calendar, and put in place whatever you need to support you in keeping that commitment.

Setting goals

When you are establishing a practice, it helps to focus on process-based goals: how much time are you spending writing rather than what you accomplish during that time. Pressure has a role in motivating your work, but working at or just beyond your limits all the time is not effective.

Success breeds success, so start with what you know you can do and then build on that gradually. You don't want to set your goal at a level where you can fail by the third week of the semester. Why would you stick to your plan if you've already failed? You also know that setting challenging goals can give you an incentive to try harder. You don't want to set a goal that's too easy.

Find the right balance by giving your goal three levels for success:

1. **The minimum:** If you don't reach this, you really need to ask yourself if you are committed to your goal. (This should feel relatively easy.)
2. **A happy medium:** You are committed and doing well. It may be a bit of a stretch but there is enough slack here for bad weeks.
3. **A stretch:** You will have to try harder but it should be achievable.

If you only set the stretch goal, there is a good chance you will not meet it and get discouraged. That's not motivating. If you only try for the minimum, you would probably feel like it wasn't really enough. That's not motivating either. By identifying all three levels, you keep the higher level of achievement in view but recognize that it might take you some time to get there.

You do not have to set goals for what you will accomplish in the time you have set aside to write. In fact, you often don't have enough information to estimate how much time any given stage of the scholarly writing process is going to take, especially when you are still developing and articulating your ideas.

Taking notes at the end of each session about how your project moved forward, what kinds of things you did, and tracking things like words written or paragraphs revised, will help you get a better sense of what you can do in a particular length of time. Allow yourself to just collect data for a while. Once you have sufficient data to work with, you can do a brief analysis to determine how much you can get done, and how much that varies, as well as what types of tasks work well in which kind of session.

I caution you against setting goals and then trying to force a certain amount or type of work in a session. Start by learning what is possible and how much it varies. Experiment with different tasks in different session lengths to work out what works best. Figure out how to make this work best for you and then use that knowledge to set achievable product-based goals.

Full Days

A full day of writing is a day when you wake up in the morning and say, "This is a writing day," and organize your activities with that in mind. Many scholars talk about full days as a sort of holy grail. It is true that having a full day with no other pulls on your time enables you to really immerse yourself in your writing, going deeper with your thoughts and possibly even losing track of time. Even when you get up from your desk to eat, or do laundry, or go for a run, your mind is focused primarily on the writing project. You can see substantial progress at the end of the day even if some of the individual sessions during the day were frustratingly slow. If this has been your experience of full days devoted to writing, then you definitely want to schedule full days in your calendar.

This is not "binge writing." Calling any long writing session binge writing is unhelpful. Binges are the kind of thing that make you sick. Binges involve doing something almost obsessively without stopping to look after yourself. Binges mean excess or lack of control. After a binge you are probably repulsed by whatever you binged on and will actively avoid it for some time. You can write for full days without binging.

The main drawback of full-day writing is that it is often difficult to find this much time for writing on a regular basis, especially during term time when you also have the demands of teaching and other work. Scheduling full days and then not writing because of the pressure of other work is demotivating. Writing for full days and then feeling like you are falling behind, or not doing your other work to a standard that you are happy with, is demotivating. On the other hand, only writing during the summer or other breaks between teaching can be unsatisfying, particularly if you take a long time to get back into your project. You may need to complement your full-day writing with other types of writing time both to make your full days more satisfying and to ensure you do enough writing to achieve your goals.

It is possible that your experience of allocating full days to writing is not what is described in the first paragraph of this section. Many people find that with a whole day available, it is harder to get down to the work and stick with it. They fritter away a big chunk of the day and are disappointed in how little they have accomplished by the end of it. It's hard enough to find full days to write. Feeling like you've wasted precious time is just going to make you feel bad.

If this has been your experience there are a couple of things you can try. The first is to structure your day. Use my suggested structure as a starting point and then adjust it to work with your own preferences. Experiment to find the best structure for you. The second, is an external structure. A writing group or writing retreat will create a focus on writing. The community of other writers will act as a motivation to stick with it. You will have less control over the form of the day and the length of the individual sessions, but this may be compensated by the benefits of that external framework and community.

It is also possible that full days are not effective for you. They are great for other people but not for you. That's okay. There is nothing wrong with you. If true, you no longer have to worry about how hard it is to find full days to write. You just need to find other ways to work writing into your schedule. You can skip right to the next chapter.

The research day

The research day is a full day each week kept clear of teaching and meetings. The advantage of this way of thinking is that it makes a clear temporal boundary between different responsibilities and sets an external guide for what the balance between those different work responsibilities should be. Setting aside your other responsibilities for a day enables you to focus more fully on your research and writing, reducing the cognitive load taken up by the juggling itself.

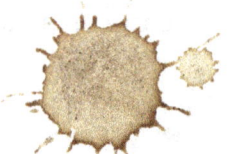

JO VAN EVERY

If this is not a feature of your own institutional culture, and you don't have this much flexibility around your teaching schedule, you can skip this section. There are other ways to incorporate full days devoted to writing into your workload.

If the research day is a feature of how your department talks about workload and timetabling, and you don't have strong evidence that full days are not effective for you, I recommend trying to make them work. To work well, you will need to put considerable effort into establishing and maintaining the boundary between research and all your other work.

You have a lot of other responsibilities and it is objectively difficult to get them all done in a reasonable amount of time. You will need to make difficult decisions about how much time to allocate to teaching preparation, grading, committee preparation, and other work and make tough decisions about the standard to which you do your other work. Be kind to yourself as you do this. Remember that your research and writing are part of your job even if the outputs and outcomes are not as immediate. The arguments you have with your own gremlins will be much more frequent and difficult than any you may need to have with colleagues.

If you find it difficult to make the research day work without feeling like you are underperforming in other areas, you don't need to take one weekly. Your goal is not only to do more writing, but to feel good about how you manage your writing time. Perhaps taking a full research day every second week would be feasible. Alternatively, you can identify weeks in which other responsibilities will be particularly heavy and plan ahead to forego your full research day in those weeks.

Setting yourself up the day before

Take some time during the working day before your research day to make the transition. The biggest threat to your research day is your other work. The objective of your transitional practice is to calm the anxiety that you are forgetting important things and remind yourself that there is a balance to be struck between your various responsibilities.

Take a moment to reflect on what you have been doing since your last research day. Set a timer for a minute or two, and make a list. Acknowledge how much effort and time you devoted to those responsibilities. Allow yourself to be pleased with what you've accomplished.

Now turn to your to-do list. Prioritize the tasks on this list. Make sure you are ready for those things scheduled for the day after your research day. If you do this earlier in the day, you can do the urgent tasks in the time remaining before you finish work. You may find it beneficial to turn on your out of office reply: "[Day] is my research day. I will address your email during normal working hours on [next working day]. Thank you for your patience."

Make a plan for when you will get to the other items, perhaps blocking time in your calendar. Also block time on the next working day after your research day to triage any email backlog. You might even consider writing a note to yourself, to read on the morning after your research day, as a reminder of your priorities. If you do your research somewhere else, tidy your desk and make it ready for the next time you come in, with your note to yourself prominently placed.

Make the space where you write inviting for your research day. Tidy away the papers that are related to your other work. Put them in folders in a drawer. Or in a storage container in a corner of the room or whatever. Take out the papers and books you will need. Put your writing to-do list in a prime spot on your desk. If you have a dedicated space you can do this at the end of your research day for the next research day.

Continuity between research days

It will be easier to devote your day to research if it is clear where to start when you sit down in the morning. The best time to decide that is at the end of the previous session. You can't do more than four to six hours of really intensive writing work in a day, so it's easy to block some time at the end of your research day to review and plan.

Start by noting how your project has moved forward. Don't restrict yourself to word counts, which may or may not be a valid measure of progress. Consider more qualitative and abstract indications of progress. Depending where you are in the scholarly writing process, those indications may relate primarily to your own understanding of the scope and depth of the project, or they may relate to how well you are communicating your ideas to your future reader.

Then list what your project needs now. Some of those needs won't look like writing. For example, you may need to read more to improve that one section. Anything that moves your project forward counts. List whatever comes to mind. Leave the list with the project so when you come back to it, you can look at the list, and pick a thing to do. Since your project needs everything on the list, you don't need to decide now, you can pick the one you most want to do the next time you sit down as a place to start. You might write Future You a short note about what you've been thinking and where you think this needs to go next. Your objective here is to give yourself a way back into the headspace you were in while writing.

If you use this physical space for other kinds of work, tidy away your research materials and get out the things you need for your next working day as a way of marking the end of your research day and setting yourself up for your other work. If this is a dedicated space, tidy the space to make it welcoming for your next writing session.

I suggest you also read "Fifteen minutes to make your longer sessions more satisfying" in the chapter "Short Snatches". You may find that ten or fifteen minutes per day between research days makes it easier to get back into your writing and makes your research day even more effective.

Writing retreats

It is difficult to find full days on a regular basis. One strategy for incorporating full days devoted to writing is to schedule them periodically and think of them as retreats. A writing "retreat" is a period of intense focus on one and only one project with lots of attention paid to pacing and self-care. I use the term "retreat" to indicate that you will retreat from your other demands (work and/or home) and focus primarily on your writing. You may or may not go somewhere special to do this.

A writing retreat has many advantages. The most obvious is that it enables an intensive focus on one writing project enabling substantial progress over a short period of time. A retreat enables you to do the kind of thinking and writing that really needs that kind of intense immersive experience. Task switching, decision making, and other cognitive tasks involved in juggling your myriad responsibilities require energy and cognitive capacity. By focusing on a limited number of activities, you reduce decision fatigue and focus your cognitive capacity in a productive way. This intense focus on one type of work can also be restful, especially when you manage your time to also give attention to basic self-care (rest, movement, food).

As Pat Thomson and Barbara Kamler have pointed out, scholarly writing is both text work and identity work.

> "As we craft a text and shape an argument, we are also crafting and shaping our scholarly self. As we write, we are enacting a particular imagined view of our selves — who we are and who we want to be."

A writing retreat also serves these two purposes. In the normal day to day of your academic life, your identity as a writer can get lost among all the other aspects of your work. A writing retreat brings this identity to the fore for a few days and can be like recharging that part of yourself in a way that sustains you through the other times.

Of course the text work you do on a retreat also provides a foundation for the kinds of text work that you find easier to incorporate in your day when also juggling teaching, other work, and your life outside of work. Make sure to incorporate strategies for making the transition from your shorter writing periods into the retreat, and from the retreat work back into shorter writing periods, perhaps building on the strategies described in the previous section. You might begin by asking yourself what your project needs and then sorting those tasks based on the kind of time that is optimal for doing them.

Solo retreats

You can go on retreat by yourself. In fact, some people prefer it. Ideally, you want to have a space dedicated to writing. Somewhere that, when you cross the threshold, you feel like you are beginning the process. That might be your home office (suitably tidied up to remove distractions). That might be your cottage. You might book a few days at a hotel or bed and breakfast somewhere.

Block off at least two days in your calendar to work on one writing project. Clear a conducive space and make it inspiring for writing. Collect your materials. Stock the fridge with good healthy snack food. Have a plan for meals. Make sure you have things that can serve as paperweights in case you decide to work outside.

Spending time setting up your space is not procrastination. The process of setting up the space is a transitional ritual. Consider what kind of environment is conducive to your writing. You might start by identifying how you would like to feel while you are working on your writing project and what kinds of work you need to do to move your project forward. That will give you clues as to what kind of setup will be most conducive. Sometimes you need to sort, tidy, and rearrange in order to create an environment in which you find it easier to write, to focus, and to enjoy the writing. You might want to have different types of spaces in which to work.

Start your day with some kind of practice that gets you moving: dance party, yoga, a long walk, a run, a bit of gardening. Alternatively, you might find that you want to start your writing as soon as you wake, and then take a break for breakfast and some movement before coming back to it. Some people find that the sort of half-awake stage can produce some really interesting insights and that once you've started writing it is easier to go back to it. Experiment to see what works best for you. **Do not, under any circumstances, start your day with email, social media, or the news. You can catch up on that later.**

Write in time blocks no longer than ninety minutes, with breaks of at least fifteen minutes between them. (If you do short 25 minute blocks, you can do 5 minute breaks but take a longer break every 90 minutes.) Get up and move away from your workspace for every break. Have a glass of water and a snack. Move your body even if it's just to stretch. You may need to set reminders or alarms. A meditation timer will have gentler sounds.

Change where you write/work if that helps. Sit in a comfy armchair. Move out to the deck. A change of scenery unblocks many a writing block. When you feel restless go for a walk (or a swim if you're at the lake). Take your handheld device (if you have one), or a small paper notebook, so you can record any brilliant thoughts that come to you. (Voice to text using Siri, Dragon Dictate, or similar software is genius for this.)

Have a real lunch break: good food, some kind of movement activity, perhaps a nap. If you are the kind of person who tends to get really into something and forgets to eat, keep protein rich snacks nearby. Finish your work day with another physical activity: a swim or a walk? Do something enjoyable in the evening. Eat a nice supper. Read a novel. Knit. Work on a jig-saw puzzle. Get a good night's sleep. Start again in the morning.

Organized group retreats

A writing retreat doesn't need to be alone. Rowena Murray has found that there are important benefits to writing in social spaces.

> "In the competitive writing culture that predominates, structured writing retreats produce cohesion in competitive cultures, create structure out of the fragments of time available for writing and build connectedness through the articulation of common goals, struggles and experiences."

The very fact that others are also devoting this time to their writing will be helpful. You will have opportunities to discuss what you are writing with other writers, whose insights may help you. And you can build a network and community of writers that extends beyond the space and time of the retreat.

A self-organized group retreat can be a good way for you and your colleagues or friends to support each other's writing. Or you can join a group retreat organized by your institution or by another organization. The group might be one you are already part of, or you might register and attend independently. The retreat may be organized specifically for academic writers or might be open to writers in a range of genres. It may be for one day or multiple days; in your workplace or in a location chosen for its difference from your normal workplace (and perhaps to be inspiring, relaxing, etc.).

You will have less flexibility in terms of how your time is structured because the structure is decided by the organizers. This can be a good thing, giving you an opportunity to experiment with ways of structuring your time and your writing that you can bring to other writing opportunities. It can also be beneficial not to have to devote any of your cognitive capacity to the organization, saving it for the writing itself. Do not dismiss retreats designed for other kinds of writers out of hand. Although scholarly writing is very different from fiction, you might find that there are ways to adapt the techniques fiction writers use in your scholarly writing. This may be particularly helpful if you've been stuck or uninspired.

It is worth talking to your Dean or your Research Office to see if they are willing to fund writing retreats. Your institution has an interest in you getting writing done and may well find that writing retreats are a good use of resources. You may also be able to use professional development funds or research grant funds to pay for the registration, travel, and accommodation to retreats organized by others.

A suggested structure for a full writing day

You probably can't do more than 4 - 6 hours of intellectually engaged writing (either creating new words or major revisions) so don't feel bad if that's the case. There are other things that will move your project forward that can be slotted into the rest of the day.

You want to build in breaks for movement and food. Even though you are engaged in mental, rather than physical, activity, you will be using energy (of the kind we measure in calories) so you will get tired and hungry. Since you are not physically moving, your muscles may get stiff. This is also one of those situations where a change may really be as good as a rest: give your brain a rest from heavy intellectual work by focusing on a less demanding task or doing something physical.

- Breakfast
- 90 minutes of writing
- 15 to 30 minute break away from your desk (with snack)
- 90 minutes of writing
- 30 to 60 minute break from your desk (lunch; physical activity)
- 90 minutes of writing
- 15 to 30 minute break away from your desk (with snack)
- 90 minutes of writing
- Stop for the day
- Plan for relaxing activities in the evening so you can get a good night's sleep.

Ninety minutes is an arbitrary number. It is probably the longest that any session should be before taking a break. Your sessions don't have to be the same length. If you benefit from writing almost as soon as you wake up, then you could start with thirty minutes of writing to get started, then break to have a shower and breakfast before coming back for a longer session. You can also break up ninety minutes into a set of shorter pomodoro-style sessions if those work well for you or for the particular writing task at hand. (Three 25-minute writing sessions with 5-minute breaks between is approximately 90 minutes.) If you work quite intensively in such a way that you lose track of time, experiment to find ways of benefiting from that flow without neglecting your need for food, water, and movement. Keep snacks on your desk. Set alarms to remind you to get up to go to the toilet and stretch.

Remember, "writing" means anything that moves your project forward. You probably want to do different types of tasks in each slot. Figure out what part of the day is best for your most creative work. Plan to do the most intensely intellectual work during that time and build the other stuff around it. Some people work better if they start with lower intensity tasks as a warm-up. Others find that they are most productive if they write first, even while not quite awake. Some people are best in the early afternoon, others find that this is the absolute worst time of day for them to do real thinking. If you are best in the evening or late at night, adjust your sleep schedule accordingly and do non-work stuff during the day. Experiment a bit to figure out what works well for you.

If you are at a stage in your project where you are doing some very intellectually demanding generative writing or major revisions, limit that kind of work to one or two of the 90-minute slots. That doesn't mean you aren't doing writing in the other slots. Reading counts. Taking notes on reading, especially if that includes writing about your own initial thoughts and reactions as well as summarizing the key points, definitely counts. Going for a long walk to really think about what you've just written and figure out what it needs next also counts. Walking around the room staring out of windows may also be part of the process. Also, organizing files (virtual or physical), tidying your desk or working space to make it easier for you to focus, corresponding with co-authors, making task lists, ordering books, or downloading articles all count.

If it moves your writing project forward, go for it. If you notice you are engaging in a task to avoid a difficult task or to reassure your gremlins that you really do have something worth sharing with scholarly peers, pause and figure out how to deal with your resistance.

Longish Sessions

You can't always find full days to devote to writing. Full days may not be effective for you. You do want to be able to get into flow with your writing and move it forward in ways that feel substantial. For most people that means at least one hour.

Your day has other things in it but you still get a significant chunk of time to devote to your writing. You can get into flow but need an alarm to keep you from losing track of time and forgetting to go to that thing you've got scheduled. Without an alarm, your brain my stay on the alert for your end time, distracting you from your writing.

This kind of time is easier to find during busier teaching terms or if you are fitting research in around other kinds of work or caring responsibilities. You might be able to do this daily, but more likely you will fit one or more sessions of this type into your week. Blocking it in your calendar is important. You may also use dedicated space or write in a group (virtually or in person). Even one session a week will result in a significant amount of writing.

You can start with the goal of getting into flow and writing until your timer goes off. If you run out of steam or get stuck, you can take a short break and then move on to a second task until the timer goes off. Or, you can decide to divide your total time into a series of shorter sessions with short breaks in between (sometimes called Pomodoros after a tomato shaped timer of that name). Some days you might do one. Some days you might do the other. It will depend on what you are working on, how you are feeling, and what kind of environment you are writing in.

Taking observational notes about your focus at the end of every session will give you the data you need to evaluate your own practice and try some experiments to see what works best for you. Remember that there isn't one right way. How you organize your session will depend on what kind of writing task you are working on, how you are feeling that day, and what's going on around you. You will get better at deciding which is appropriate in what circumstances with experience.

Daily writing for one hour or more

If you can devote at least five hours per week to writing but you either can't clear a full day of other responsibilities or don't find full days effective, you might try daily writing sessions of an hour or more. Like the research day (see section in the previous chapter), devoting this much time to your writing every day even during busy teaching terms requires tough decisions about how much time you spend on your other responsibilities and the standard to which you do your other work. If you work in a research intensive institution with a relatively low teaching load, this is probably possible. If you work in an institution with a relatively high teaching load, it may not be. If you are not writing anywhere near this much in term time right now, you might want to work up to it using a combination of weekly long sessions and short daily writing, gradually extending the length of your daily writing sessions. (See "Fifteen minutes to build a habit" in the next chapter.)

You will need to adjust when you schedule your daily writing time to account for what is possible in terms of scheduling teaching or meetings you are required to attend. Daily writing sessions may be easiest in the morning, before going to the office. If you are able to request that your own teaching (and meetings) not be scheduled before 10 or 11 a.m., you can even fit long daily sessions into a normal work day. If that is not possible, you will need to adjust your sleep schedule so you can get up very early so you don't get derailed by teaching or meetings scheduled in the early part of the normal work day. Early morning writing is also popular for writers in all genres who have a day job that doesn't involve writing.

Morning is popular partly because having already written changes the way your whole day feels. Writing in the morning takes "priority" quite literally and makes writing the first thing you do in a day. That said, not everyone finds morning writing effective. If you are a night owl, you might prefer scheduling your daily writing in the evening. This may still require you to rearrange when your normal work day starts to enable you to get enough sleep. Carving out an hour or two in the middle of the day may require more boundary maintenance and learning to write in your office, but can also be effective.

You will need to put effort into establishing and maintaining the boundaries of this time. Block the time in your calendar so you have a visual reminder that this time is allocated to writing and not available for other activities. If you use a shared electronic calendar make sure the event is set to "Busy" so no one thinks you are available for meetings. You can be flexible about this time when necessary, but be confident about the legitimacy of blocking it off in this way. (See the section "Fifteen minutes as emergency practice" for ideas.) If you are routinely skipping writing to do other things, you need to either find a better time-slot or re-evaluate whether you can really manage this amount of daily writing.

Is once a week enough?

If you cannot fit daily writing sessions of an hour or more into your schedule, don't panic. There are lots of valid reasons this may be the case. A writing practice is not an all or nothing thing. Making writing a priority does not mean devoting more time to it. It means making some time available for it.

Even one longish session per week will make your writing more satisfying in a context where it is difficult or impossible to do more. You can get into flow during that session and make recognizable progress on your project. If you are able to write for ninety minutes per week every week for a 12-week semester you will have done eighteen hours of writing. This is not a negligible number. Even if you have to skip your session a couple of times due to the pressure of grading or some other periodic task, you're likely to get at least fifteen hours of writing in during term time.

You may be able to fit more than one session of this length into your workload at least in some weeks. You are looking for a balance that enables you to get writing done without feeling like you are underperforming in other areas of your work and life because of it. If one session is all you can do, start there.

It will be easier to establish this habit if you are able to have your long session at the same time each week. Schedule your weekly writing sessions a semester at a time, marking them as "busy" in your electronic calendar. Then organize other meetings around them. For extra support, you can also participate in virtual or in-person writing groups if the times work with your other commitments.

If you are able to devote more time to writing during the summer break, a weekly long session will provide continuity throughout the academic year, and make next summer's writing more effective. You won't have the extra work of remembering where you were and trying to get back into it; you can just increase the number of hours devoted to writing. If you have a reading week in one or both semesters, you could supplement your weekly sessions with a full day (or two or three) during the reading week.

You may find that the demands of your other responsibilities mean that you can only fit in one long session per week, and you devote the first part of every long-ish session to remembering where you were and getting back into it. This can be frustrating. In this situation try combining your one long session a week with daily very short sessions. (See "Fifteen minutes to make your longer sessions more satisfying" in the next chapter.)

A suggested structure for a one to two hour session

Clear your desk of anything not related to your writing (you can just put it in a drawer or a storage box temporarily; or cover it with a towel or sheet), or use a space in which you only work on your research and writing. Turn off your email program. Put your phone on Do Not Disturb (which has a setting that allows your child-care provider or other named number to get through in an emergency). If you are writing in your office, put a Do Not Disturb sign on your door.

- Stretch gently, with a particular focus on your shoulders and wrists.
- Pick a project to work on.
- List everything this project needs to move forward.
- Pick something to start with. And a second thing to have in reserve.
- Decide how you will optimize your focus taking into account, the nature of the task, how you are feeling today, and the context in which you are writing.
- Set your timer and write.
- When your timer goes off, stop writing.

Take some brief notes about how your project moved forward, what it needs next, and perhaps some obser-vational notes about your focus. Put your writing things away, take your sign off the door, switch your phone back to normal, and move on to whatever is next.

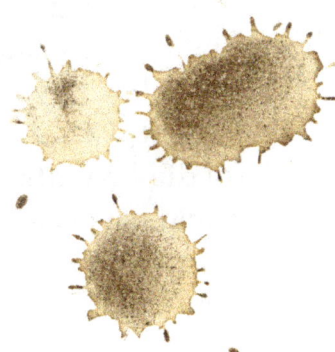

Short Snatches

When I say short, I mean short. I use the term "snatches" deliberately because sometimes you really are just snatching a bit of time in a very busy day. It's a lot easier to find ten to thirty minute chunks of time than full hours or full days.

What you can do in short snatches of time is limited but you may be surprised by how much you can do. These short snatches of time add up. Even though any one of them seems kind of pointless, if you commit to using them, you may find that you get a lot more done overall. There are lots of tasks that move your writing projects forward that will work well in ten to thirty minutes. I encourage you to try it.

You can plan for short writing sessions as a minimum engagement with your writing on busy days. You can also grab them when they appear. They may even be indeterminate lengths of time in which you need to be interruptible. This kind of time is everywhere if you keep a notebook with you at all times or have a smartphone. You might use an app like Evernote to organize short bits of digital writing or you might prefer a paper notebook and have a system for incorporating handwritten notes into your workflow

In the sections that follow I will use fifteen minutes to stand in for this short amount of time. It doesn't have to be fifteen minutes. It can be ten, or twenty, or thirty. It's just easier to write one number. The important thing is that it's short. Probably so short that you think it's pointless. It's not. There are lots of different reasons to use short sessions.

Fifteen minutes to build a habit

If you would like to have a daily writing practice but don't have one now, fifteen minutes is a good place to start. Your goal isn't to get lots of writing done, it's to build the habit of writing at a particular time of day every day. Once you have a habit, you can work on extending the amount of time you devote to it every day, as your schedule allows.

By starting with a really short block of time, you don't have the excuse that you don't have time today. No matter how busy you are, you can take fifteen minutes to work on your writing without throwing the rest of your day off. Other people can wait fifteen minutes for whatever they need you for. If you end up going to bed fifteen minutes later, or deciding to wake up fifteen minutes earlier, it won't make a huge difference to how much sleep you get or how tired you feel.

Because you are building a habit, you probably want to think about what time of day you would like to do your daily writing in the medium to long term. This might be your best time of day for intellectually demanding or creative work. It might be the time of day you are mostly likely to be able to keep clear of teaching commitments. It might be a time of day when your kids don't need you (e.g. before they get up or after they go to bed). Don't worry about this too much. Just pick a time of day to begin with.

Building habits is easier if you peg your new habit to a habit you already have. Now that you have a broad sense of the time of day, what other things do you routinely do at that time of day? Do you want to write immediately after a meal (perhaps with coffee in hand)? Right after your shower? As soon as you get into the office? You are looking for something you do every day around the same time of day that you want to write, preferably something you don't really think too hard about. You're going to use that established habit to anchor your new writing habit and create a chain. Here are some examples of what that could look like:

Wake up, shower, get dressed, **write**, eat breakfast.

Wake up, **write**, shower, get dressed, eat breakfast.

Wake up, get coffee & toast, **write**, shower, get dressed, have more breakfast.

[Morning routine], go into the office, lock door behind you, **write**, unlock door, get on with day.

[Morning... through to about noon], eat lunch, **write**, [afternoon]

[Normal day], come home, **write**, make dinner, etc

[Normal day], come home, [normal evening], put kids to bed, **write**, something relaxing, go to bed.

Figure out what will normally come before your writing session. You can modify one of the examples to suit or build your own.

If you write in the same place every time that will help too. However, you also want to be able to keep your habit even if you are away at a conference or whatever, so you can make this a bit more flexible. Where are you at this time of day? What options do you have available to you?

You may also find it helpful to pre-decide what you are going to work on. You can keep a running list of things you could tackle in short snatches of time with your various writing projects. Ask yourself "What does this project need to move forward?" Write down everything that comes to mind, no matter how ridiculous. Break down the bigger things on that list into the smallest possible pieces. (e.g. "Rewrite paragraph 6 on page 3 to better express ..." vs. "Edit the draft"). Since your goal is to build the habit, you probably don't want to pick a project you have a deadline for, though you can use this time to do pieces of that deadline project in addition to other time you might spend on it.

Habits are hard to establish. It is likely that you will miss days for one reason for another as you establish this habit. You don't want to give up the first time this happens. You want to stick with this long enough to really figure out if you can make it work. There are a couple of ways you can approach this. Your personality will dictate which one to try. Whichever method you choose, remember you can restart any time.

If you are you the kind of person who really likes streaks, there are a number of habit tracker apps that will allow you to keep track of whether or not you've done your fifteen minutes. You can decide whether "daily" means working days only or x days per week. You aren't committed to a seven day per week practice if you don't want to be. Only choose this method if having a long streak motivates you to do the thing even when you don't want to so you don't break your streak.

If you are the kind of person who is more likely to give up the first time you skip a day because you've broken your streak than to be motivated not to skip in order not to break your streak, then that method is probably not for you. I recommend that you use the three level goal method outlined in the Planning chapter.

This is all about the process. You probably also want to keep track of what you do but try to do so for observational purposes only. Your goal is to establish a habit of writing daily. What you do is much less important than that you do it. If you are sitting down and doing something that moves a writing project forward for fifteen minutes a day, you are on track.

Fifteen minutes to make your longer sessions more satisfying

One of the arguments against very short sessions is that you can't do anything satisfying in such a short period of time. Shorter sessions may not be satisfying in and of themselves, but they can make those longer sessions more satisfying either by keeping you engaged with the project so you get back into flow much more quickly when you have more time available, or by moving all the fiddly, not very satisfying, parts of the project along so that you can devote your longer sessions to the more intellectually satisfying parts of the process that really benefit from more time.

Writing isn't just generating new text. Getting your text from first draft to published involves a lot of fiddly little tasks that don't really need long, uninterrupted sessions. In fact, sometimes it's hard to stay focused on these tasks for a long time and you split your longer session into a series of short ones anyway. Think of short sessions as a complement to your longer sessions. The more unsatisfying tasks you can do in short snatches of time, the more satisfying your long sessions will be. Those little bits of work will add up to something significant even if any one short session doesn't feel like much.

There is another reason your long sessions might be unsatisfying. You may only be able to find time for one longer session each week. You are so busy the rest of the week that, every time you sit down to write for that one long session, you have to remind yourself what the project is about and where you are and what you wanted to do next. You may have scheduled ninety minutes, but feel like you only really get sixty. Given that this is the only writing time you have, you get discouraged. If you aren't able to find a long session weekly and are reliant on writing retreats between teaching terms and during reading weeks, it's been even longer since you last looked at your project. You can feel like you are taking two steps forward and one step back.

Newton's first law of motion (inertia) seems to apply to the non-physical world, too: It takes more energy to get a stopped project started than to keep a project moving. When your longer writing sessions are infrequent, you spend considerable energy (and time) getting back into the project, reducing the amount of time available to be in flow and advancing the project. Imagine if you got into things quickly and could spend most of your 90 minutes in flow?

Instead of thinking of short sessions in terms of how much you can get written, think about them as keeping you engaged with your project. Try adding short sessions on the other days of your working week, or adding in a fifteen minute per day habit (see previous section) between retreats. Your goal is to keep your project from grinding to a complete halt. No matter how slowly it's moving, you want it to keep moving so you don't have to apply that extra force to get it going again.

Fifteen minutes to overcome resistance

Have you ever had a project where you wanted to work on it but also didn't want to work on it. Maybe it just feels too daunting? Maybe the subject matter is emotionally difficult and the thought of spending an hour or more in that emotional place is creating some resistance even though you know it's an important project and you want to get it out there. Maybe you have a revise and resubmit you need to work on, but the thought of looking at the reviewer comments is causing some panic.

The very short session is ideal in this situation. By setting a very tiny goal, you correspondingly reduce the resistance to something you can easily push through. If you only have to do fifteen minutes, it's easier to convince yourself to open the project and start. Once you've started, you might keep going, but that's not a requirement. You don't get to chastise yourself if you only do fifteen minutes.

The trick to making this work well is to make your fifteen minutes absolutely compulsory, either seven days a week or every working day. You must give this project fifteen minutes (or whatever short amount of time you decide) no matter what. If you are getting ready to go brush your teeth and put your pyjamas on and you haven't done it yet, you have to stop and do your fifteen minutes before going to bed.

If you have the time available and you want to stay open to the possibility that you might be able to do more than fifteen minutes, use the stopwatch feature on your phone rather than the timer. You could also write down the time you are allowed to stop as a comparison point for when you look at the clock. This way, if you happen to get into flow, you won't be interrupted by an alarm going off. If you find yourself looking at your timer frequently, you know exactly when you can stop.

In some situations you may define your minimum commitment by something other than time. You can break down a big task into its smallest components and then set your goal based on these tiny increments. For example, if it's a revise and resubmit that you are avoiding, you can define your first session as "open the comments from one reviewer and skim them." That's enough. Your next session might be to open the comments from a second reviewer. Maybe the first reviewer's comments are not as bad as you thought, so you decide to keep going. Because your goal was to open only one set of comments, you have already achieved your goal and can stop anytime. Do not set a new goal mid-session! If you open that second set of comments and the first paragraph is in a tone that triggers all your anxiety, you are allowed to stop and do it tomorrow. You might also send it to a friend to read and summarize for you.

This strategy might take you right through to the end of this project. You might also find, at some point, you've done enough that you don't feel the same resistance to working on it when you schedule a longer session. Trust yourself. Your goal is to keep your project moving forward. If you find that your resistance is mainly because your project is at a stage where it's just not that motivating but you need to devote more time to it because it needs to be finished, the next strategy might help.

Fifteen minutes for a different project

Remember, the scholarly writing process isn't just about producing publications. It's also about using writing to articulate, develop, and organize your thoughts. Every scholarly writing project generates new questions that don't really fit but might become new projects. You also get ideas from your teaching, from talking to your colleagues, or from other things you are reading or doing. Sometimes those ideas can be distracting. Like toddlers, if you ignore them they keep poking at you. While they don't fit into the current project, you also don't want to forget about them.

You can use short snatches of time to "dump" the ideas that are swirling around in your brain into a notebook so you can focus on your main project. This is low stakes writing. The ideas in your Dumpster file/notebook may turn out to be not as exciting as you thought. Or, they may develop into a really interesting and important project. It really doesn't matter in the moment. Writing about them is valuable in and of itself.

There are several ways to incorporate this use of short snatches of time into your writing practice. This can be what you write during the fifteen minutes you are using to build a daily practice. Even when you have a longer practice you might find doing this kind of writing first thing in the morning makes it easier to come back to writing later in the day. You can start a longer session with a timed short free-write as a way to warm up. Once you've started writing, you can carry that energy into your main project.

You can also use this strategy when other ideas come to you while you are working on your main project. By pausing to write down that other idea, you can relax back into your focus on the main paper. You won't forget about it, and you can give it real time and attention later.

A special instance of this situation is when you are coming to the end of a project. The tasks that remain are usually not the most exciting ones, and you can get into a bit of a perfectionist spiral where you spend a lot of

JO VAN EVERY

time fixing tiny things in an attempt to calm your fear of what reviewers will say. The inertia problem can also appear as a kind of resistance to finishing to avoid the extra energy starting a new project takes. Although you enjoy writing, you don't have to enjoy every aspect of it. You may well need to push yourself through your main project to get it finished.

Just because your main project deserves more of your writing time and energy, doesn't mean you have to make yourself hate writing. Giving small amounts of time to a new exciting project can be beneficial. You get to devote some time to something more stimulating than checking references. You get the next project started without any real pressure to ramp it up or do anything substantial with it. After a while, all those short snatches of writing on the new project start to turn into something interesting enough that you really want to get the almost finished project off your plate so you can really dive into it.

Tips for using this strategy:

- Use a timer as a way to prevent this off-project writing taking your focus away from your main project altogether.

- Even five minutes can enable you to get enough of an idea down that you can come back to it later.

- You may want to have a notebook, Evernote folder, or document where you keep all these short pieces of writing.

- Develop a routine of periodically looking back through what you've written, grouping ideas, and making decisions about what you want to pursue further.

- You may also notice that some ideas don't really hold your attention over time and that others are persistent, which is helpful when thinking about your research and publication strategy.

Fifteen minutes as emergency practice

Although significant parts of your work during the main part of the academic year are scheduled weekly or relate to things scheduled weekly, your workload is not as consistent as your teaching schedule might suggest. There are periods of more intense activity at the beginning of term, and when assignments come in. During these periods, you might find it harder to protect your writing time. There are also unpredictable changes to your schedule. An opportunity arises that requires immediate action. You (or your kids) get sick. Your car breaks down. Even with slack in your schedule, you may have to adjust your workload to deal with whatever it is.

It's okay if you can't do much writing (or any) for a week or two. Sometimes other things really are more important and more urgent. Trust your judgement. You don't need to waste time and energy juggling balls that you could put aside. And you certainly don't need to waste time and energy worrying about dropped balls, or doing weird gymnastics trying to pick those balls up without dropping anything else. It is better to make a conscious decision about how to adapt your writing process in this circumstance.

One option is to drop back to fifteen minutes a day. It's enough to keep you engaged and stop you worrying but not so much you drop other balls. If writing is important to you, being able to keep it going, even in a crisis, may be calming. Make a conscious plan for how much time you can devote to writing and schedule it. Don't let your gremlins tell you that's not enough. In fact, if you are worried you can't do even that much, make it less.

I also recommend doing your writing first. You can even do it before you leave for the office (while you drink your coffee). You can then go do whatever else you have to do knowing you have already written. Don't worry about how much you write, just do your allocated amount every day and then put it away. If you get more writing related ideas on your way to work, have a way to record those as notes but only record them as notes.

Trying to "squeeze it in" requires more cognitive energy and creates a lot more emotional processing. If morning is not your best time, give writing your BEST time of day. And schedule it. For example, if you know you are best in the middle of the day, allocate time for writing at lunchtime. (Eating lunch, and leaving your office to walk to somewhere to eat lunch and write for a bit, will also be worthwhile.)

Remember that this is temporary. This is not a typical week. You will have your more normal weeks again. You can even mark the date on your calendar when you can give more time to writing.

Figure Out What Works for You

If scholarly writing is important to your work or your identity, you must prioritize it and find time in which to work on it regularly. This is always difficult and depends a lot on your job description, your institution, and the organizational culture. Making writing a priority doesn't necessarily mean giving it a lot of time. It means giving it resources of time and energy before other things.

This *Short Guide* has described three different kinds of writing time and described different ways you can use each kind of time. You will need to experiment to figure out what works best for you but it will probably involve some combination of all three.

Making writing a practice that you engage in regularly, whether or not you have a specific output with a deadline, will enable you to engage in all stages of the scholarly writing process. It will remind you regularly that you are a writer. It will transform how you feel about your work.

Enjoy your writing!

Notes & References

Everyone struggles with making time for writing: I discuss the separation of writing as a process from writing as a product in more detail, and provide details of the different stages of the process, in *The Scholarly Writing Process* (ISBN 978-1-912040-72-8 ebook; 978-1-912040-00-1 pb), the first volume of the *Short Guide* series.

I also recommend Helen Sword's *Air and Light and Time and Space* (2017, Harvard University Press). It is based on research with successful academic authors and provides a detailed analysis of their practices. Sword offers a framework for constructing a writing practice based on four habits: Behavioural, Artisanal, Social, and Emotional. A web resource for finding your BASE can be found here: WritersDiet.com/base.php

Gremlins are my word for the voices in your head that try to give you advice or comment on what you are doing. They seem to think bullying is a motivational technique and sarcastic comments are helpful. Mostly they are trying to protect you from failing, making a fool of yourself, or whatever. They have a tendency to be overprotective so they often accidentally "protect" you from succeeding, too. There is a downloadable colouring page on my website that may be helpful for dealing with them: jovanevery.ca/gremlin-colouring-page/

Planning to include writing: I have written more about planning in *The Principles of Juggling: A Picture Book for Academics* (ISBN 978-1-912040-71-1) and on my website: JoVanEvery.ca/elements-good-plan/ (with links to further posts on specific issues).

The definition of "priority" is from the *Shorter Oxford English Dictionary* (6th edition, 2007)

The leveled goal setting strategy I describe is adapted from a strategy a client successfully used.

Full days: The term "binge writing" seems to originate in the work of Robert Boice, who wrote several books on academic writing practices based on his own research and experience in faculty development including *Advice for New Faculty Members* (2000, Allyn & Bacon). He is careful to distinguish binge writing from any long period of writing but those drawing on his work seem to be less careful. For an example of what binge writing looks like, and how it contrasts to a healthier writing practice, I recommend this blog post by Lisa L Munro: "Writing As Self-Care" (December 6, 2015 LisaMunro.net/blog-1/2015/12/6/writing-as-self-care). An alternative to the binging vs snacking metaphor that circulates can be found on my website: JoVanEvery.ca/hiking-metaphor-for-summer-writing/

The biggest impediment to setting an out of office message and not dealing with email during your research days or writing retreat is fear of the deluge on your next working day. "Email Triage" from *Productive Flourishing* (ProductiveFlourishing.com/email-triage/) is a useful technique for managing email.

The Pat Thomson and Barbara Kamler quote can be found on page 19 of *Writing For Peer Reviewed Journals* (Routledge, 2012). They refer to the content of the writing and I extend it here to the process.

The Rowena Murray quote on the value of group writing retreats can be found on page 72 of *Writing in Social Spaces* (Routledge, 2015). I recommend Murray's book for more information about group writing activities of various types. In particular, Appendix F offers a suggested structure for a 2-day retreat.

For one example of how your writing might progress over a several day writing retreat, Pat Thomson has written a blog post about her "Two Week Book Chapter:" PatThomson.net/2017/02/20/my-four-day-book-chapter-a-k-a-down-the-writing-burrow/

Aimée Morrison has written about what she can write in a day at *Hook & Eye*: HookandEye.ca/2018/02/07/how-much-can-i-write-in-a-day/

For ideas on how to make a case for funding or organizing writing retreats to your Dean or other institutional gatekeeper see Yolande Strengers and Cecily Maller's post at *The Research Whisperer*: theResearchWhisperer.wordpress.com/2017/03/21/ writing-retreats-academic-indulgence-or-scholarly-necessity/.

My suggestion that you not write in blocks longer than ninety minutes is primarily based on what's good for your physical body. You may think of your work as primarily intellectual, but your brain is in your body. You need your shoulders, back, wrists, etc to be functioning optimally to be able to write. Look after your body. Get up and move regularly. You can observe what length of time seems to work best for you and adjust your schedule accordingly.

Rachael Herron talks about "breaking the seal", writing even a little bit before you do anything else to make it easier to get back to writing later in the day, in Episode 60 of her podcast *How Do You Write* (RachaelHerron. com/ep060/)

Longish sessions: I've written more about focus on my website JoVanEvery.ca/focus-and-distraction-self-flagellation-not-required/ .

Raul-Pacheco Vega has written about how he gradually shifted his sleep schedule to enable daily early morning writing: www.RaulPacheco.org/2016/08/why-did-i-switch-to-starting-work-at-4am-and-how-did-i-do-it/ Note: he has a napping couch in his office and takes a long nap in the early afternoon as well as going to bed reasonably early. This strategy is not about working more hours. If you'd like some virtual community. there also seems to be a Twitter hashtag for writers (all genres) who do this: #5amwritersclub

I host a virtual writing group as part of the Academic Writing Studio (JoVanEvery.ca/mwyw). There is a virtual Shut Up & Write Tuesdays group meeting on Twitter: suwtuesdays.wordpress.com/about-2/

There is a Writing in Progress door sign at the back of this book for you to photocopy. You can also download one in either US Letter or A4 format from my website: JoVanEvery.ca/15-min-writing-challenge/#resources

The suggested structure is based on the structure of A Meeting With Your Writing, the virtual writing group I host as part of the Academic Writing Studio (JoVanEvery.ca/mwyw).

Short snatches: Raul Pacheco-Vega shared an example of the surprising amount you can do in fifteen minutes on Twitter. See this tweet and those in the thread before and after: twitter.com/raulpacheco/status/924248068094136320 .

Evernote (evernote.com) is one popular notes app that many people use and that integrates well with other writing tools. I mention it as an example. Any app that allows you to write short chunks of text will work. You can also dictate notes into your phone and either transcribe them later or use voice-to-text software to convert them.

Raul Pacheco-Vega's Everything Notebook posts are all linked here: www.RaulPacheco.org/resources/the-everything-notebook/ . You can also find information about Bullet Journals and other strategies for keeping a notebook with a quick internet search but beware of the Pinterest rabbit hole. Your goal is to find ideas you can try, not to find the perfect analog to-do list and note keeping method.

I created the 15 minute/day academic writing challenge (JoVanEvery.ca/15-min-writing-challenge) to help you build a writing practice from the smallest building blocks.

Habit tracker apps: If you have one you like for other habits, just add your writing to it. Two that I have heard of people using are Good Habits and Habitica. LifeHacker has a review post on apps for iPhone here: lifehacker.com/the-best-habit-tracking-app-for-iphone-1791778063. Veronika Cheplygina has written about integrating Habitica with a to do list app here: www.VeronikaCh.com/habits-productivity/how-to-use-both-todoist-and-habitica-without-syncing/.

If you want a pen and paper method for tracking habits, there is also a free downloadable tracking sheet on the 15 minute challenge page of my website (JoVanEvery.ca/15-min-writing-challenge/#resources) Or, add a tracker to your Bullet Journal or Everything Notebook if you use one.

Acknowledgements

I developed the strategies in this Short Guide over many years. I have published earlier versions of some sections as blog posts on my website. Some of those posts are edited substantially for inclusion, others remain more or less unchanged. I thank everyone who responded to those posts for helping me clarify and develop my ideas.

I am particularly grateful to Jennifer Hofmann's Inspired Home Office and Creative Haven, where I learned a lot about organizing time and space, about self-compassion, and about hosting online classes and work sessions. Jennifer has moved on to a different kind of work, but her approach to decluttering and office organization, and the community she built in the Creative Haven, have influenced both this book and the Academic Writing Studio.

Some of the ideas presented here were first elaborated in the classes I run as part of the Academic Writing Studio, though those classes predate the consolidation of various things into the Studio. Establishing a Writing Practice and Planning Your Semester (or your summer) all include some of these ideas.

The Short Snatches chapter started out as a series of blog posts, was developed into the 15 minute/day Academic

Writing Challenge, and developed further as those who took the challenge shared with me how they used it. I would also like to thank Rebecca Raphael for her "what I do on my sabbatical" Facebook post (November 2017) in which she talked about "The Dumpster".

Thanks to Dalie Giroux for telling me how she used ten minutes of writing a day to overcome resistance and complete a project. Hosting A Meeting With Your Writing since 2011 has given me plenty of evidence of the value of the Longish Session. Thank you to my clients, whether participants in a Meeting With Your Writing, coaching clients or participants in various workshops, for everything you have taught me about the variety of things that work.

I am grateful to many conversations on Twitter about academic writing, both those I participated in and those I observed. The #acwri and #getyourmanuscriptout hashtags are particularly helpful for learning more about the wide variety of strategies that work for scholarly writers. Raul Pacheco-Vega, Pat Thomson, Inger Mewburn, Katherine Firth, and Helen Kara are generous with their advice and ideas though they are by no means alone in supporting academic writers on Twitter and through their blogs. The fact that a particular person or blog is not named in no way indicates that it did not influence my approach or that they are not worth following or reading. I have also learned a lot from Rachael Herron's "How Do You Write" podcast.

The scholarly writer I observe most also cooks me dinner and generally makes it possible for me to do this work, even when it isn't quite paying the rent. Thank you for your support, Matthew Paterson.

Thanks to the Alliance of Independent Authors for advice and support on self-publishing and to Helen Kara for pointing me in their direction. Thank you Amy Crook for graphic design, Sarah M. Lacy for virtual assistant support, Bonnie Zink for editing the manuscript, and Rohan Maitzen for comments on a draft.

I'm sure I'm leaving people out due to faulty memory, a desire for this section not to surpass the main content in length, and uncertainty about where to draw the line. I value all of my friendships virtual and in real life, and I'm sure they have all influenced the person I am today and my ability to write what I have written here.

About the Author

Jo VanEvery transforms academic lives from surviving to thriving. She used to be an academic sociologist and then a program officer for a funding agency. Now she helps you juggle your myriad responsibilities, provides a structure so you can get more writing done, helps you clarify your vision and make a plan for the next part of the path towards it, and boosts your confidence so you can do the work that makes your heart sing. You can read more of her writing on her website, JoVanEvery.ca; follow her on Twitter, twitter.com/JoVanEvery; or like her Facebook page, www.facebook.com/JoVEAcademicCareerCoach/ .

Also by Jo VanEvery:

The Scholarly Writing Process: A Short Guide (ISBN 978-1-912040-72-8 ebook; 978-1-912040-64-3 pb)

The Principles of Juggling: A Picture Book for Academics (ISBN 978-1-912040-71-1 pb)

Praise for The Scholarly Writing Process

"Reading *The Scholarly Writing Process*--I'll be recommending it to #acwri and #thesisbootcamp people! I really like the distinction between writing as process and writing as outcome." Dr Katherine Firth, Lecturer, Research, Education and Development, La Trobe University. Co-founder Thesis Boot Camp.

"Insightful, accessible & excellent. Read now! The advice was superb and got me itching to be writing for the first time in a while." Simon Cook, PhD Researcher in the Department of Geography, Royal Holloway University of London and Lecturer in Academic Skills at Birmingham City University

Coming soon:

Scholarly Publication: A Short Guide

Peer Review: A Short Guide

Saying ~~No~~ Yes: A Short Guide

Writing

Meeting

in

Progress

Please Do Not Disturb

CPSIA information can be obtained
at www.ICGtesting.com
Printed in the USA
LVHW060024180619
621555LV00007B/23/P